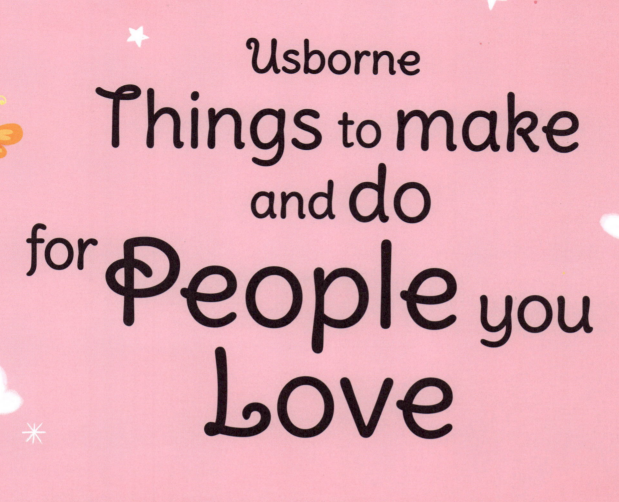

Usborne
Things to make and do for People you Love

Designed by Kate Rimmer and Carly Davies

Illustrated by Manola Caprini,
Manuela Berti and Krysia Ellis

Words by Kate Nolan

Always ask a grown-up to help with cutting, or any other tricky things.

T0406036

Make a heart suncatcher

Tape it to a window so that the light shines through.

1 Cut a piece of baking or tracing paper to use as a base.

2 Tear tissue paper into small pieces.

3 Stick the pieces of tissue paper all over the base.

4 When it's dry, fold it in half.

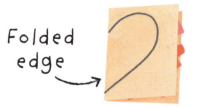

Folded edge →

5 Draw a shape like this...

6 ...and cut it out.

7 Unfold.

Use any tissue paper you like.

2

Make a heart bouquet picture

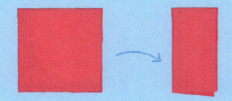

1 Cut a square of paper about as wide as four fingers. Fold it in half.

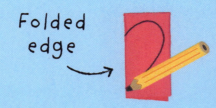

Folded edge

2 Draw a curved line like this...

3 ...then cut along the line and unfold.

4 Do steps 1–3 again to make more hearts.

Leave space at the top.

5 Draw two crossing lines on paper.

6 Add more lines between them.

Heart at the top of a line

7 Put glue on one half of a heart, then stick it on. The other half will pop up.

Some can overlap.

8 Repeat step 7 until each line has a heart at the top.

Draw friends holding hands

1

Draw two heads...

2

...and two bodies.

3

Add arms and legs.

4

Draw hair and faces.

Draw more pairs
of friends on
this page.

Make a ribbon reward

...to show someone how much you appreciate them.

1 Flatten two cupcake cases.

2 Put glue in the middle of one, and stick the other on top.

Rectangles as wide as your finger

3 Cut two narrow rectangles of paper.

4 Stick them to the back of the cases.

5 Cut a small circle of bright paper and stick it on the front.

Add a smaller case in the middle if you have one.

6 Draw or stick on decorations.

You could cut the ends of the paper strips.

Make pencil toppers

...for your friends and classmates.

1 Draw a straight line on paper like this.

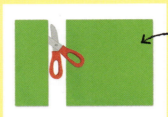

You don't need this bit.

2 Cut along it.

Don't cut right to the edge.

3 Make lots of cuts along the paper.

4 Glue halfway along the uncut edge.

Start from the unglued end.

5 Wrap the paper tightly around a pencil...

Press the glued end down.

6 ...until you reach the end.

7 Curl the ends of the paper.

8 Use a pen to add a face.

Print a teddy bear card

...to send a bear hug to someone you love.

1 Fold some thick paper in half.

Paper towel

2 Cut a large potato in half. Dry the cut side.

3 Dip the cut side in paint...

4 ...then print it on the paper.

5 Dip the tip of your finger in the paint. Print two ears...

You could use a smaller potato to print baby bears.

6 ...and four paws.

7 Leave to dry, then use pens to add details.

Make a pop-up flower card

Send love to someone with these heart-shaped blooms.

About the length of your finger

1 Fold a sheet of thick paper in half.

2 Make two cuts in the middle like this.

3 Open the paper up and push the flap inside...

  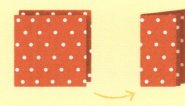

4 ...then press it down.

5 Cut two squares of bright paper, a bit wider than the flap.

6 Put them on top of each other and fold in half.

Two folded hearts

Folded edges together

7 Draw a curved line like this...

8 ...then cut along the line and separate.

9 Tape the hearts together like this.

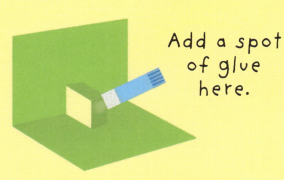

Add a spot of glue here.

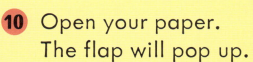

10 Open your paper. The flap will pop up.

Tape is at the back.

11 Press the heart onto the glue.

12 Stick on leaf shapes cut from paper.

You could stick on a bee like this, or any other decorations.

Draw on details with your pens or crayons.

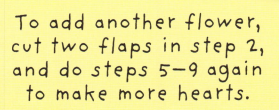

To add another flower, cut two flaps in step 2, and do steps 5−9 again to make more hearts.

Make wrapping paper

This printed paper is perfect for wrapping gifts.

Fingerprint hearts

1 Pour a little paint onto a paper towel or some newspaper.

2 Dip your finger into the paint.

3 Press onto a sheet of paper...

4 ...then print again to make a heart shape.

The prints overlap at one end.

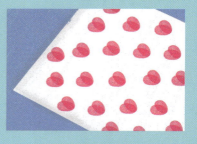

5 Cover your paper with hearts.

You could draw on faces after the paint dries.

Cardboard tube print hearts

Pinch the other fold into a point.

1 Flatten a cardboard tube.

2 Push one of the folds in like this...

3 ...and use tape to hold it in a heart shape.

Spread the paint out.

4 Pour a little paint onto a paper towel or some newspaper.

5 Dip the end of the tube in the paint...

6 ...and print on paper.

You could print a gift tag too.

11

Make a sock bunny

1 Cut the band off the top of an old sock.

2 Stuff the sock with cotton balls...

3 ...then close it with an elastic band.

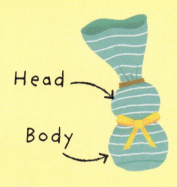

Head

Body

If you don't have a ribbon, use the cut-off sock band.

4 Tie a ribbon around the middle.

5 Make a cut in the top of the sock.

6 Glue the layers together on each side.

Glue on a cotton ball for a tail.

7 Snip each piece into an ear shape.

8 Draw on a face using a felt pen.

You could stick on a pompom nose instead.

Draw a bunny

1 Draw a head and a body.

2 Add two long ears.

3 Draw a face...

4 ...two lines for legs, and a tail.

Draw more bunnies on this page.

Make paper beads

...for a bright necklace to give as a gift.

Newspaper

1 Put blobs of paint on a sheet of paper.

2 Put another sheet over the top.

3 Smooth it out to spread the paint.

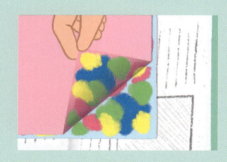

4 Peel the two sheets apart...

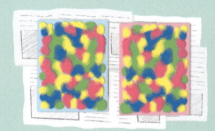

5 ...and leave to dry.

6 Cut the paper into strips, then cut the strips in half.

7 Cut a long point at one end of a strip.

Don't glue this end.

8 Put glue on the back...

If you want to make wider beads, cut wider strips.

9 ...then curl it around a pencil.

Repeat with all your strips.

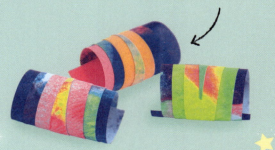

How to make a necklace

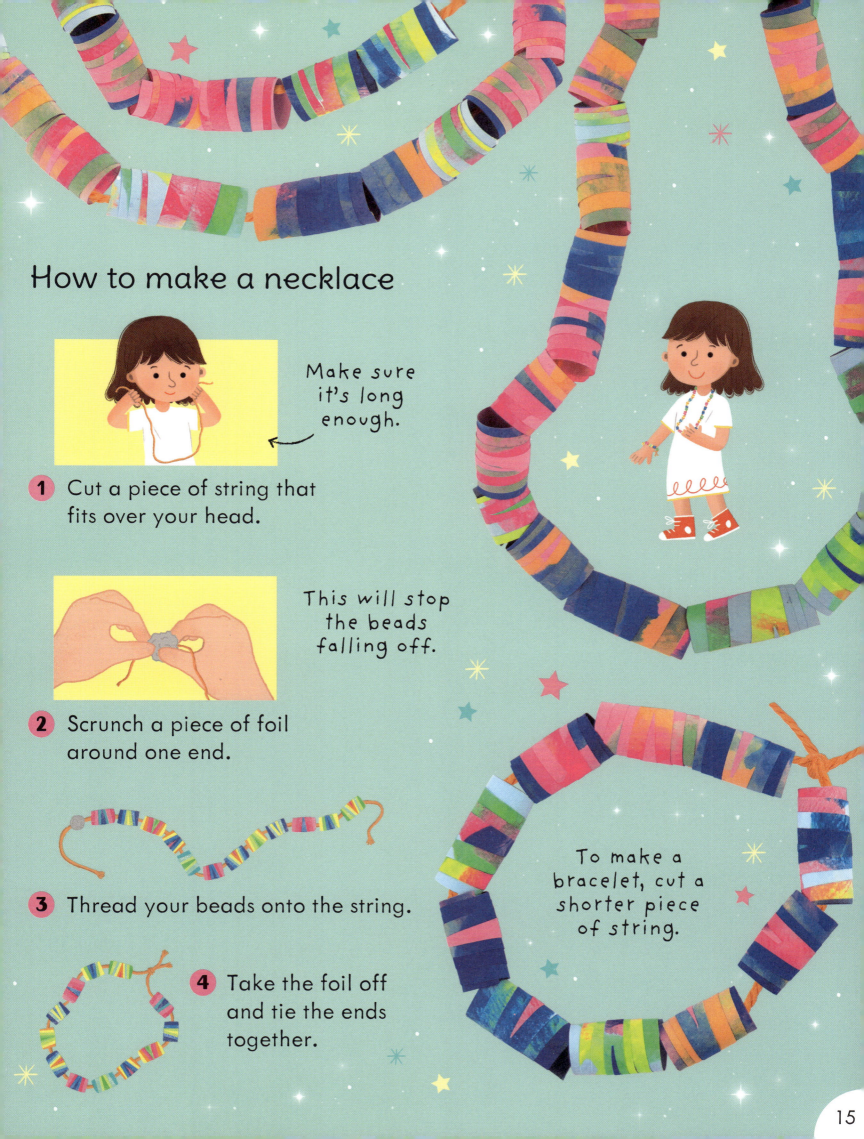

Make sure it's long enough.

1 Cut a piece of string that fits over your head.

This will stop the beads falling off.

2 Scrunch a piece of foil around one end.

3 Thread your beads onto the string.

4 Take the foil off and tie the ends together.

To make a bracelet, cut a shorter piece of string.

Make a flower fan

1 Put a bowl on paper, draw around it, and cut out the circle.

Not too wide

2 Make a fold near the edge of the circle.

3 Turn it over and fold it the other way.

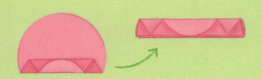

4 Keep turning and folding until you get to the end.

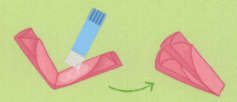

5 Fold it in half, add glue, and press together to stick.

Two hearts

6 Open out, then do steps 1–5 again to make another heart.

7 Stick your two hearts together.

8 Flatten the tip of a paper straw...

9 ...then glue it in where the two hearts join.

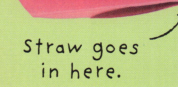

Straw goes in here.

Draw a flower

1 Draw a stem.

2 Add a petal on each side.

3 Draw one more at the top...

4 ...and add a leaf.

Draw lots of flowers.

Make gift packages

This is a fun way to wrap small presents.

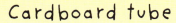

Cardboard tube

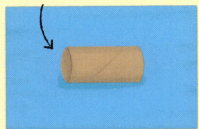

1 Cut a piece of wrapping paper.

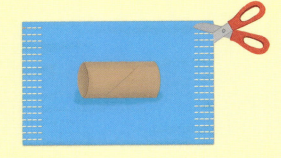

2 Make lots of cuts down the sides.

3 Put glue on the top and bottom edges like this.

4 Stick the tube to one of the glued edges.

5 Roll the paper around the tube.

See how to cut out hearts on page 3.

6 Press the other edge down to stick in place.

7 Scrunch the paper at both ends.

8 Tie one end with string or ribbon.

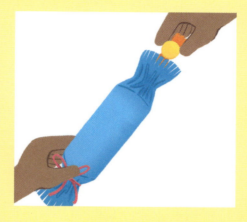

9 Put the gifts in...

10 ...then tie up the other end.

Paint or print your own paper if you like.

You could snip out triangles in step 2.

Make a heart

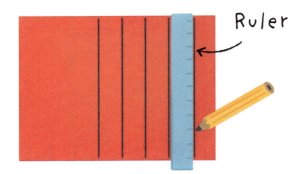

Ruler

1 Draw five straight lines on paper, about the same width apart.

2 Cut along the lines to make five strips.

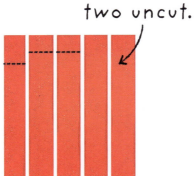

Leave two uncut.

3 Cut three of the strips like this.

Shortest strip in the middle

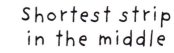

4 Glue the strips together at one end like this.

Outer strips will bend out.

5 Glue the ends of the outside strips together.

Glue

Stick here.

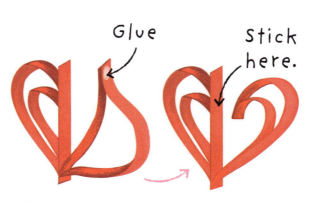

6 Bend the ends of the strips over. Glue them to the middle strip.

String   Tape

7 Add a loop of string to hang.

Make a flower wristband

You could paint your tube first.

...to give to a friend.

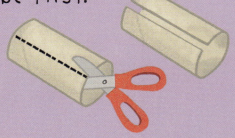

1 Cut all the way down a cardboard tube...

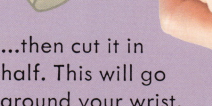

2 ...then cut it in half. This will go around your wrist.

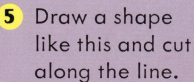

3 Draw around a cup on bright paper and cut out the circle.

4 Fold the circle in half three times, like this.

5 Draw a shape like this and cut along the line.

Slit

6 Open it out and stick it to the band.

Stick a smaller flower on top in step 6 if you like.

7 Scrunch up some tissue paper and glue it in the middle.

Make pipe-cleaner roses

1 Peel apart five sheets of toilet paper, to make ten sheets.

2 Put them in a stack. Draw around a mug on the top one.

3 Cut out the circle, through all the layers.

4 Fold the stack of circles in half.

5 Make two small cuts in the middle.

6 Open out. Thread a pipe cleaner partway through one cut.

7 Bend it back down through the other cut and twist the end.

8 Lift the first layer of tissue and scrunch it.

Use tissue paper instead if you like.

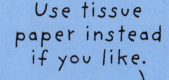

9 Keep lifting and scrunching, one layer at a time.

You can buy pipe cleaners in craft stores.

Make a friendship chain

1 Fold a piece of paper in half...

2 ...and in half again.

You can use both pieces.

3 Cut in half this way.

4 Draw a head and a body.

5 Add arms and legs that go right to the edges.

6 Cut around the outline, without cutting the folds.

7 Open up your chain...

8 ...and add details.

Draw a love bird

1 Draw a body.

2 Add a heart for wings...

3 ...and three lines for a tail.

4 Draw an eye, a beak, and feet.

Draw more birds flying around this page...

...and some perching on the branches too.

24

Make cupcake-case birds

...with heart-shaped wings.

1 Flatten two cupcake cases.

2 Fold and glue them both in half.

3 Fold one of them in half and half again.

4 Draw a curved shape like this and cut it out.

Wing

5 Unfold it once to make a heart shape.

6 Stick the other case on a piece of paper.

7 Glue the wing on top like this.

8 Use a felt pen to add details.

Make as many birds as you like to fill your paper.

Make a paper tulip

A gift of flowers is a lovely way to brighten someone's day.

1 Cut a square of paper as wide as your hand.

2 Fold it in half like this and trim the edges.

3 Fold one corner up...

Two tulips

4 ...then the other corner. Then do steps 1–4 again to make another tulip.

5 Glue the back of one of the tulips.

6 Stick on a straw, then press the other tulip down on top.

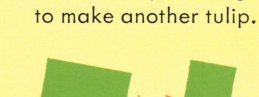

7 Cut a smaller square of green paper. Fold it in half.

Leaf

8 Draw a curved line. Cut along it, then unfold.

9 Stick the leaf to the straw.

Use your pens or crayons to make these postcards bright, then cut along the dotted lines and give them to people you love.

Write the name of the person you're giving it to, and sign your name underneath.

To

Love from

To

Love from

Make a sunshine flower

...for your friend to tape to their window.

1 Draw around a small bowl on paper.

2 Cut out the circle.

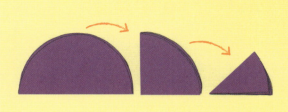

3 Fold it in half three times.

Snip off the tip.

4 Draw curved lines like this and cut them out.

5 Open out the circle.

6 Draw around the same bowl on tissue paper.

7 Cut out the circle...

8 ...and stick it behind the first circle.

Make a flower pot

A pot of paper flowers makes a perfect present.

 Remove the lid if it has one.

1 Wipe a recycled container clean.

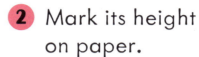

2 Mark its height on paper.

3 Cut a strip that fits around it. Cover with glue...

See how to make these tulips on page 26.

4 ...then stick it on.

5 Put a spot of glue near the top.

 Glue on mini pompoms if you like.

6 Stick on one end of some string or yarn.

7 Wrap it around your container...

8 ...and glue the other end down near the bottom.

9 Do steps 6–8 again until it's all covered.

Page 22 tells you how to make these roses.

If your pot is watertight, you could use it for real flowers, too.

Make a love bug

Paint your bug after step 2 if you like.

1 Tear or cut a cup off an egg box...

2 ...and trim the edges.

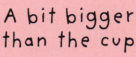
A bit bigger than the cup

Wings

3 Use a pen to add a face.

4 Cut a square from paper. Fold in half.

5 Draw a curved line like this. Cut along it, then unfold.

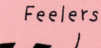
Feelers

6 Draw spots on the wings.

7 Cut two small strips of paper and curl the ends.

8 Stick the wings and feelers on.

You could use patterned paper for the wings.

Draw a love bug

1 Draw a body.

2 Add a heart for wings...

3 ...and a line for the head.

Draw more bugs flying around this page.

4 Draw on a face, legs, and feelers.

Make a bright butterfly

...to give to someone you love.

1 Fold a sheet of paper in half.

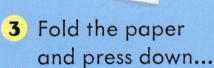

Only on one side

2 Open it out and add blobs of paint.

3 Fold the paper and press down...

4 ...then open. Let it dry.

Use a wooden stick as a guide for the wing size.

5 Fold over again and draw a wing shape.

6 Cut it out.

7 Unfold...

8 ...and glue the stick in the middle.

9 Draw a face.

Feelers

10 Glue two strips of leftover paper to the back of the stick.

You could make the wings a different shape.

Fill in the stick with a felt pen if you like.

Make pebble pals

Paint a pair of friendship pebbles for you and your best friend to keep.

Soapy water

1 Wash two pebbles that look similar and let them dry.

2 Paint them...

3 ...and leave them to dry.

4 Use paint or pens to decorate them.

Use one of these ideas, or think of your own.

Love bugs

See how to make fingerprint hearts on page 10.

You could do the same design in different shades.

36

Use your pens or crayons to make these postcards bright, then cut along the dotted lines and give them to people you love.

Write the name of the person you're giving it to, and sign your name underneath.

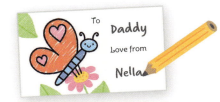

To

Love from

To

Love from

Make a cupcake card

...to send to a friend on their birthday.

Slanted sides

1 Fold a sheet of thick paper in half.

2 Cut a shape like this out of old wrapping paper.

3 Stick it near the bottom of the card.

Flame

4 Draw a candle in the middle.

5 Put glue around the bottom of the candle...

6 ...and press cotton balls onto the glue.

You could draw on extra details, too.

Make a rainbow mobile

This is a lovely gift to brighten up someone's day.

Make a sun...

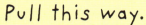

Pull this way.

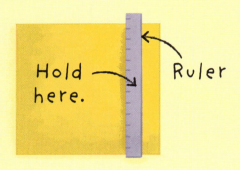

Hold here.

Ruler

1 Hold a ruler down straight on yellow or orange paper.

2 Tear four strips from the top.

3 Draw around a cup on the leftover paper...

4 ...and cut out the circle.

5 Tear your strips in half. Stick them around the edge of the circle.

6 Draw on a face, then stick a string to the back.

...then raindrops...

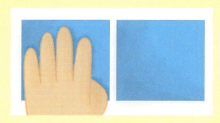

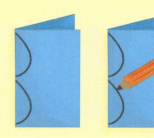

Two raindrops on each

1 Cut two squares of blue paper as wide as your hand.

2 Fold each square in half. Draw on curved shapes like this.

3 Cut them out and unfold. Stick them onto two strings.

...and a rainbow.

1 Draw around a plate on paper. Cut out the circle.

2 Fold it in half, then cut along the fold.

3 Draw a red stripe around the top edge of one piece.

4 Fill your rainbow with more stripes like this.

5 Cut out the white part from the middle, then stick a string to the back.

Tie your sun and rainbow strings onto a stick.

Tape your raindrop strings to the back of your rainbow.

Draw a butterfly

1 Draw a body.

2 Add two wings on one side...

3 ...and two wings on the other side.

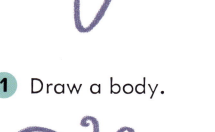

4 Draw a face and feelers.

Draw more butterflies on this page. When you make the flower picture on the next page, you could decorate it with butterflies too.

Fingerprinted flowers

1 Lay down newspaper and put paper on top.

Green crayon

2 Draw lines like this for flower stems.

Not too much paint — spread it out.

3 Put small blobs of paint on a paper towel.

4 Dip your finger into the paint...

5 ...then print it around the stems.

Wash your finger before you use another paint.

You could print petals around a middle like this.

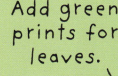

Add green prints for leaves.

Make a fun frame

If you want to give someone a picture you've made, it's nice to frame it.

1 Cut a sheet of thick paper bigger than your picture.

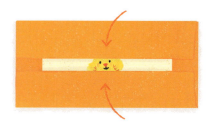

2 Fold the top and bottom edges over the picture...

3 ...then the sides.

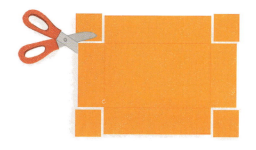

4 Unfold, then cut a square out of each corner.

5 Decorate the edges however you like.

6 Turn it over so the blank side faces up.

7 Glue your picture in the middle.

8 Roll one edge around a pencil.

9 Repeat with the other edges, so the decorations show.

You could frame a picture you've made from this book.

Add stickers if you have some...

...or glue on shapes cut from bright paper.

Send a hug in a card

Perfect for a birthday, or any day!

Save one for later.

1 Fold two sheets of thick paper in half and open them out.

2 Paint your right hand with a brush.

3 Print it on the right-hand side of one sheet.

Opposite side

4 Do steps 2–3 again with your left hand.

5 When it's dry, cut along the fold.

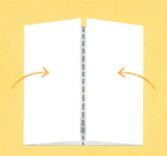

6 Fold the edges of the other sheet so they meet in the middle.

7 Turn it over so the flaps are underneath.

8 Bring the edges in to meet the middle line.

9 Press the flaps down. Put glue on them...

10 ...then stick on your handprints.

11 Open the card and draw a picture of yourself inside.

Make sure your arms join to your hands.

You could draw or stick on extra details.

Send a secret message

1 Fold a sheet of paper in half...

2 ...and in half again.

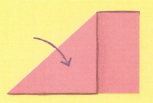

3 Fold the top corners down to meet the bottom edge.

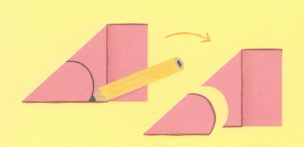

4 Draw a curved line like this and cut along it.

5 Open it out and write your message in the middle.

I love

You could use wrapping paper if you like.

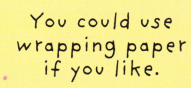

6 Fold it back into a heart shape, ready to give to whoever you like!

I love you

48